The Knights Templar

The

Knights

Templar

The Hidden History of the Knights Templar: The Church's Oldest Conspiracy

Conrad Bauer

ISBN-13:978-1519488763

Printed in the United States

Contents

Introduction 1

The Savagery of the First Crusade 3

    Protection for Pilgrims 5

    Preparing for the Crusade 9

    Arriving in the Holy Land 11

    The Battle for Jerusalem 13

Formation 17

    Foundation of an Order 19

    Growing the Coffers... 23

    Endorsement from the Pope................................. 27

    Becoming the Bankers 31

The Downfall 35

    The Squadron Charge 39

    The Second Crusade.. 41

    Leaving the Holy Land 45

    The King of France 49

    Dissolution 51

    The Templar Fleet 55

    Fleeing to Scotland.. 57

    A Stop in Portugal... 61

    A Local Rebellion... 63

Relics 66

    The Temple of Solomon 67

    The Copper Scroll.. 71

    The Turin Shroud... 73

    The Ark of the Covenant...................................... 77

    The Holy Grail.. 81

De Molay's Curse... 93

The Freemasons 103

Legacy... 109

Conclusion 113

Further Reading 115

About the author.. 117

    More Books from Conrad Bauer 118

Introduction

The Knights Templar existed officially for less than 200 years. Founded to protect pilgrims who were traveling through the Holy Lands, their rise to power was sudden. They became some of the most feared warriors in the region, they had a mandate from God, they controlled perhaps the world's first real banking system, and they waged war against anyone who tried to wrestle Christianity's holiest grounds from the control of the Catholic Church. Within their short lifespan, they quickly became one of the most powerful societies in Europe, if not the world.

But, just as they rose to power with relative speed, they fell from grace just as fast. Forged in the crucible of Middle Eastern conflict, their power was soon resented and feared. Before they could become even more powerful, the greatest nations in Europe and the Church turned on them. The once powerful Templars were hunted, caught, tortured, and eventually burned at the stake. According to their prosecutors, they were a devil-worshipping secret society who spat on the cross and plotted against the Pope. They were officially disbanded and their members treated with extreme contempt and prejudice.

Or so goes the official story. In this book, we will not only look into the official history of the Knights Templar, but will examine the various ways their influence and ideas have tunneled their way into the modern world. A group this powerful does not vanish overnight. Instead, their history has been linked to the Freemasons, to vicious curses, to the butchery of the Crusades, and even to Christian relics such as the Holy Grail. For many people, the Templars did not vanish and they did not relinquish their tight grip on the power structures of medieval Europe. Instead, they went underground. Read on to discover the dark and twisted secret history of the Knights Templar.

The Savagery of the First Crusade

It is important to understand the context in which the Knights Templar were founded. Their formation was not as simple as a group of knights agreeing to gather together under one banner. Instead, their order was forged in the midst of the violence, conflict, and religious turmoil that was the medieval Holy Land. Much like our world today, the Near East of the turn of the first century was not a calm place. For centuries, it had been the area from which many of the world's major religions had been formed. The three huge Abrahamic religions – Judaism, Christianity, and Islam – were all born in the same area. Indeed, they share many of the same principles, historical figures, and even religious texts. With all three religions deriving from the same geographical location, the fight for supremacy in the region led to constant conflict.

To Western readers, this conflict is most familiar through the Crusades. From the Christian perspective, the Crusades were a series of military campaigns waged in the Near East and divinely sanctioned by the Catholic Church. At the time, Islam controlled much of the region and Christian pilgrims were struggling to find safe passage to the holy sites they wished to visit. Christianity was facing a major schism, as the collapse of the Roman Empire had led to divisions forming between the Western head of the Church in the Vatican in Rome and his Eastern equivalent in Byzantine (the city later known as Constantinople and eventually Istanbul.) According to historian Paul Everett Pierson, Pope Urban II not only saw the first campaign as a chance to protect Christians in the Holy Land, but as a chance to reunite the disparate branches of the Church back under his control.

Protection for Pilgrims

The first Crusade was prompted by a letter sent from the Byzantine Emperor Alexios I in 1095. Alexios begged the Pope for assistance, knowing that the head of the Church might be able to rally an army in order to protect the citizens from around the world who were attempting to make the journey to holy sites in cities such as Jerusalem as these citizens were often finding themselves in trouble. Though the Muslim rulers in Palestine and throughout the Holy Land nominally allowed for Catholic pilgrims to journey through their lands without an issue, this was not always the reality. The crimes supposedly committed by the Muslim rulers in the Holy Land were violent, vicious, and offensive to Christian sensibilities. These included suggestions that the Turks who controlled the area had ravaged the churches belonging to Christians in the region, that they had captured the city of Christ (Jerusalem) and had blasphemed against it by selling the Christian institutions (government offices, shops, merchants, tax offices, etc.) into abominable slavery, and that they had been harassing, bullying, and even committing acts of violence against the good Christians who simply wished to journey to the land of their savior.

As with many proclamations calling for violence and war, however, these claims were likely exaggerated. Emperor Alexios was himself facing a difficult reign, his Byzantine Empire having to disband their standing army following economic worries and the inflation of their currency. He needed help projecting power in the region, so turned to the place where his empire had traditionally been associated: Rome. He begged the Pope for assistance, for the military liberation of the region, and for help in turning back the wave of Muslim rule imposed by the conquering Turks.

In November of 1095, the Catholic Church held a conference to determine whether or not to assist Alexios. The Council of Clermont is documented in a number of different contemporary texts, by a number of writers who may have been present at the Council. The accounts do not tell the same story. Robert the Monk – who was present – suggests that Pope Urban decreed that it was God's will to intervene in the region. In return, Robert writes, the Pope promised absolution (forgiveness for mortal sins) to the men who would become crusaders. Other sources have suggested that the Pope instead offered an indulgence (an award that would reduce the punishment for any sins committed.) However, all of our accounts remember that the Pope focused more on the conquest of the Holy Lands, rather than providing assistance to the Byzantine Empire. It was agreed that the mission would be put into motion on the 15th of August, a date important in the Catholic Church. Led by Adhemar of Le Puy, the first Crusade would set out on the same day as the Assumption of Mary.

Preparing for the Crusade

In a pre-Reformation Europe, the Catholic Church held a monopoly over religion. All Christian doctrine and its interpretation flowed through the corridors of Vatican City. While only a small district within the once-powerful city of Rome, the Vatican's power was on a similar level to that of France, Britain, and the other major countries. At the time, however, the Church had no standing army. If they were to launch a Crusade – a military campaign – then they would need soldiers. Not only would they need troops to fight, they would need men to lead. As such, Pope Urban issued his decree to the countries around Europe and requested that they send men of high and low birth to fight on behalf of the church. As well as the soldiers, a preacher named Peter the Hermit gathered together a group of 20,000 pilgrims and began the journey to the Holy Land.

But they did not travel far before they became embroiled in controversy and religious warfare. In 1096, as the 20,000 pilgrims passed through the Rhineland in Germany, they came across the cities of Worms, Speyer, Cologne, and Mainz. At the time, these cities had large Jewish communities. Such was the religious fervor of those embarking upon the First Crusade, that these Jewish communities presented an easy target for the mob's pent up wrath. As well as this, it was their first chance to practice their violence on a large scale. Bands of both knights and peasants who were traveling with the group became increasingly violent as they encountered Jewish communities. This violence included attempts at forced conversion, beatings, torture, and execution.

Perhaps the most violent of these early Crusader armies was the one lead by Count Emicho. Under his authority, a group of 10,000 Crusaders – both nobility and peasants – began to slaughter Jewish communities in large numbers. Though many of the local clergy objected – as did the Catholic Church itself – there was little that could be done to stop the marauding bands of Crusaders. Communities of 800, 900, and even 1,000 were killed. Sources tell of one Jewish man who, after being forcibly converted to Christianity, was so overcome with the guilt of his actions that his killed his entire family and himself. One woman, hoping to escape the cruel violence of the Crusaders, killed her entire family before they could be subjected to the whims of the massed ranks. For historian David Nirenberg, the events of late 1096 planted the seeds of violent anti-Semitism which would eventually grow into the horrific slaughter of the Holocaust. The Rhineland massacres – as they came to be known – were an early indication of the kind of religious warfare promised by the Crusades.

Arriving in the Holy Land

The main army of the Crusaders was composed of French and Norman knights, backed up by soldiers from across Europe. They fought under the banner of the Church, with up to 100,000 men journeying to Byzantine to wage their war. Because they fought for a religious cause, the Church was able to offer them spiritual rewards. The importance of promises such as indulgences or absolution meant that not only would crimes committed during the Crusades be forgiven, but that sins already committed at home were less likely to deny the perpetrator entrance into the kingdom of heaven. For those who fervently believed in the Christian faith, this was a cause they could get behind.

Once the forces had gathered in modern-day Istanbul, the Crusade could begin in earnest. It was not a short campaign, lasting for many years. One of the first major conflicts came when the Crusaders tried to take the city of Antioch and laid siege to the city. Though the residents lasted almost a year behind the walls, they eventually fell to the Crusaders. Once inside, the Christians offered no quarter in their treatment of the Muslim population. They slaughtered them, soldiers and civilians both. The sacking of the city was so complete that a Muslim army was able to creep up on the Crusaders and lay siege to the city themselves. The Crusaders rallied their troops within Antioch and went out to meet the army being led by Muslim commander Kerbogha. They triumphed and held on to the strategically important city.

The Battle for Jerusalem

From Antioch, the majority of the Crusader army marched south. Their goal – as it had been from the start – was to take the city in the name of Christianity. At the time, it was under Islamic control, but the city's population of Jews were able to live and practice their religion in relative peace. Even visiting Christian pilgrims were permitted to visit the holy sites and pray. This was not enough. Jerusalem was to be under Christian rule and the Crusaders would fight tooth and nail to wrest the city from their enemy's grasp.

Both the Muslims and Jews within Jerusalem fought long and hard against the Crusaders. But they would not hold out forever. On the 15th of July, 1099, the Christians took control of the city. What followed was a massacre. Much like at Antioch, the Crusaders pillaged the city. Anyone found to be a Muslim or a Jew was killed. Civilians were slaughtered en masse. The buildings that had been erected by Islamic architects were torn down, from mosques to other civil institutions. For one Crusader, Raymond D'Aguilers, the massacre was vindicated. He wrote a book titled 'Historia Francorum qui ceperunt Iherusalem,' in which he describes the Christians' entry into the city. His description of the Temple Mount

13

suggests that the Crusaders' butchery was so great that blood rose to the knees of the men as they rode their horses.

Another source – Fulcher of Chartres – tells of 10,000 citizens being slaughtered, including women and children. Others report that the stench of the dead bodies was so great that they had to be carried beyond the city walls and left to rot outside. The funeral pyres, we are told, were so big they resembled pyramids. Only God alone could know the true number of men, women, and children killed that day.

Following the capture of Jerusalem, the Crusaders had control of four major cities in the Holy Land. These were Antioch, Tripoli, Edessa, and — the jewel in the crown — Jerusalem. For historians such as Riley Smith, however, the result of the First Crusade was not simply the territory now under Christian control, but the 'wave of pious, Catholic fury' which had been unleashed. The various massacres stretching from Germany to Jerusalem were indicative of the extent to which the Catholic Church's armies were able to use violence to achieve their goals.

After this campaign of violence, it seemed as though the Church had been at least partially successful. The Crusade had provided a banner under which Christians could unite and had exhibited the military power that the Church was able to project. For Christian pilgrims, passage to the Holy Land was now much safer. With Tripoli and Antioch both lying close to the Mediterranean Sea, the journey to Jerusalem could be conducted along Christian-held routes. But while protection for these pilgrims had initially been a goal, it had been supplanted in the name of control. Passage for Christians was not enough; now, they had to hold on to the Holy Lands.

Following a period of fearsome, church-backed violence, this was the world into which the Knights Templar would emerge. Already tainted by the violent butchery of the First Crusade, the blood of the massacres would linger over their formation and dictate their doctrine from their very first moments.

Formation

The Knights Templar were formed in a world of religiously motivated slaughter and butchery. It is perhaps fitting that an organization so embroiled in secrecy and rumor was founded at a time when trying to discern right from wrong, and fact from fiction, was so incredibly hard. When we look into the formation of the Knights Templar, it is difficult to tell the facts from the legend.

In 1099, following the capture of Jerusalem, it became more and more common for pilgrims to want to make the journey to the Holy Land. From all over Europe, those who were dedicated to the Christian faith (and those who could afford it) traveled from Britain, France, Germany, and other countries to visit the sites where Christ had lived and died. The First Crusade had been fought to restore this territory to the Catholic Church's control and they had succeeded in taking a number of important cities. But the land between the cities was not under their control. If anything, they had managed to make the environment even more hostile to the presence of Christians. Thanks to the bloodlust of the Crusaders, people across the Holy Land began to bear a grudge against them.

Bandits and highwaymen were regular threats to those pilgrims who sought to make the journey to the sacred sites. After the Crusaders had elevated the levels of violence in the region, there was little to prevent these locals from killing the Christians they came across, and these journeying Christians were sometimes killed in their hundreds. Despite one of the initial goals of the Crusade being to protect these travelers, they had failed. By the time 1119 rolled around, something needed to be done. Christian authority in the cities they controlled had been cemented enough that a king had been installed in Jerusalem – King Baldwin II – and a patriarch named Warmund assisted him.

Foundation of an Order

The idea of the Knights Templar was suggested by a French knight named Hughes de Payens. The proposal was for the creation of a dedicated, monastic group of knights who would use their military abilities to protect the Christians traveling from Jaffa to the interior sites of the Holy Land. The Church's support was not instant, but the Council of Nablus held in 1120 approved the idea. The Knights Templar was formed and King Baldwin II provided the order with their headquarters, located in one of the wings of the Royal Palace on Templar Mount. This was previously part of the Al-Aqsa Mosque, said to be built on the original site of King Solomon's temple and one of the places where the Crusaders had shed the most blood during their invasion of the city. This mystical location would forever be linked to the order.

The new collection of knights named themselves the 'Poor Knights of Christ and the Temple of Solomon.' This was often shortened to simply 'Templar Knights' or 'Templars.' At the beginning, there were nine members. As well as Hughes de Payens, Godfrey de Saint-Omer and Andre de Montbard would be important founding members, while their numbers also included Payne de Monteverdi, Archambaud de St. Agnan, and two other knights known simply as Gondamer and Rossal. One important bond shared by the founding members was that they were all related, whether by blood or marriage. To this day, we still do not know the identity of the final, ninth knight.

The Knights Templar, as a brand new order, found themselves with very little financial backing, hence the inclusion of 'poor' in their title. In order to really drive this point home, their emblem was drawn as two knights sharing a single horse. This impoverished, monastic existence would be a far cry from the Templar's later years.

Indeed, life in the early years of the Templars soon became anything but impoverished. One of the order's chief backers was a leading figure in the Catholic Church, named Bernard of Clairvaux. Bernard was not only a powerful French abbot, but he was the nephew of Andre de Montbard. He backed the order from the very start, writing letters to other authority figures praising the new Knights Templar. With blessings like these, the Templars soon gained a very valuable standing in the Church, becoming a favored charity. This formal endorsement from the religious figures of Europe meant that they were now able to receive donations of money, land, businesses, and other financial enterprises from backers throughout Christendom. As well as this, the order could take in the sons of noble families to swell their ranks. For aristocrats who wanted to help in the Crusades but did not want to take part themselves, a son could be dispatched to serve in the Knights Templar and it would be treated as a great honor.

Growing the Coffers

The growth of the Templars' coffers is one of the key factors that people point to when discussing the shadowy nature of the organization. During the first nine years of their existence, very little is known about the group. Despite the known presence of biographers and writers in the Holy Land – specifically in Jerusalem – at this time, they are notably absent from many of the primary sources we have from this time. This lack of evidence is taken by some people as being indicative of an active suppression of discussion about the Templars' activities. There is no doubt that the group was quickly noted for their importance, as they were permitted to house themselves in the Temple of Solomon, one of the holiest of sites in one of the holiest of cities in all of the Christian world. That they should not be present in histories and descriptions of the time, according to some, is evidence that their existence was not allowed to be discussed. This is a difficult theory to prove, however, and few historians or academics lend the idea much credence. However, as we begin to look through their history and notice their sudden accumulation of wealth, power, and reputation, we should consider why they went through such a notably fallow period during their early years.

During those first years, the Knights Templar remained largely silent. They faced criticism at first, including arguments from people who suggested that truly religious men would never be able to carry a sword. But their intentions and objectives were praised by various members of the clergy and soon the arguments began to die down. One of the key defenses of the group involved the idea of a 'just war,' that is, a war intended to defend the Church from violence. Over time, the Templars began to resemble an order of warrior monks. Bernard of Clairvaux wrote in defense of the 'fearless knight,' whose soul would be protected by an 'armor of faith,' who would fear 'neither demons nor men.' From the outset, the Templars were permitted their use of violence in order to accomplish nominally Christian gains. Based in a temple noted for the Muslim bloodshed, with their violence ordained by the Church, the Templars' numbers began to grow.

Their fame was also spreading throughout Europe. Their goal of defending the Christian faith against a Muslim invasion (however unlikely this was) was not only limited to the Holy Land. On hearing about the order, Portugal's Countess Teresa promised the Templars Soure Castle in the south of the country. Soure was close enough to North Africa that the reigning European monarchy feared that they may be caught in a pincer movement, with Islam threatening Christianity on two fronts. Needless to say, the Templars took charge of the castle as a part of their burgeoning land holdings. Similar lands and finances were gained in 1131, when Count Ramon Bereguer III gave to the Templars his border stronghold named Granyena, near Barcelona. In 1134, they gained their biggest donation yet when King Alfonso I of Aragon died and bequeathed his kingdom to the order. Shortly after, they expanded their control over the Amanus March (the area surrounding Antioch) and were given lands in England. Templar-owned properties and fortifications were appearing all across Europe and the Near East.

Endorsement from the Pope

Another huge benefit came in 1139, when Pope Innocent II decreed that the Knights Templar were to be considered exempt from local laws. The rulings of the Church superseded local governance, so this allowed the Templars to pass from one country to another without needing permission, pay taxes, or bow to any authority other than the Pope, so this decree gave them a huge amount of power. Now, the Templars were almost an international organization, able to move across Europe at their pleasure and work throughout Christendom in their mission to defend the pilgrims who were traveling to the Holy Land.

Throughout the early years of the order, some of the most important records we have of their existence relates to their trail of legal documents. Not only were the order being given properties throughout Europe, but they were beginning to make purchases themselves. We have documents from the period suggesting that the Knights Templar purchased property in 1122, 1123, 1125, and 1126, as well as many more in 1127 and 1128. These purchases were made possible thanks to donations, but it was not just money, livestock, property, and land that was donated. Some aristocrats, upon their passing, left behind a set amount of labor from their indentured serfs. This provided the Templars with access to a number of workforces. Because they could move freely between countries and were not to be subjected to any taxation (on Papal orders), the wealth of the Templars was exponentially rising. Within two decades of their founding, without the modern communications networks enjoyed by modern businesses, the order had properties and chapters throughout Europe, including stations in France, Scotland, Spain, Portugal, and England, as well as their bases in the Holy Land cities. As suggested by numerous historians, including Karen Ralls and Michael Benson, the Knights Templar could be considered the first multinational corporation in the history of the world.

With power and wealth came influence. The fame of the Knights Templar grew and grew. Despite their original aim being to protect pilgrims as they traveled across the Holy Lands, they were soon a cornerstone of a Crusader military in the Holy Lands. With bases across the region and support and members arriving from the richest, most powerful families of Europe, the Christians in the region depended on this cadre of organized, educated knights to lead the vanguard of the defense of the most sacred sites. John Robinson describes the Templars as the 'largest standing army in the Christian kingdom'. An order which had first been formed under the guise of poverty and chastity soon found itself the favored charity of the Christian world, with riches flooding into its coffers. Thanks to the wealth they had accrued, the Templars began to embark on an enterprise which may actually have led to their downfall.

Becoming the Bankers

Armed with a papal endorsement and a freedom from taxation, the Templars found themselves ideally positioned to become a bank. Any members joining the order took vows of poverty and donated their possessions to the Templars. Added to the gifts from others, donations, business dealings, and loot from military campaigns, the poverty-sworn monks found themselves with both a large amount of wealth and the ownership of a powerful, recognized international infrastructure. This allowed them to position themselves as a trusted institution, a place that the nobles of Europe would be able to use in legal dealings or as a bank.

For example, when a nobleman wished to join the Crusades, he might be away from his home for a number of years. He could entrust his wealth and power to the Templars and place his business dealings under their control. In their trust, it would all be safe for him to reclaim when he returned. Within a short time, the majority of the Templars' manpower was not dedicated to military roles, but to their financial wrangling. Their mission changed. Traditionally established to protect those traveling to the Holy Lands, their aim was now to protect the wealth of these pilgrims. They could even issue a form of credit, setting up the system which would evolve into what we know today as a modern bank. Any pilgrim visiting a Templar institution in his home country could deposit money or valuables and be issued a letter noting what they owned. This letter could be presented at any other Templar holding and would allow the pilgrim to withdraw money from the amount they had deposited. Without the need to carry around their wealth, the pilgrims were less of a target for bandits and attackers.

A key element of Templar success in this regard was their ability to communicate in code. When writing letters to one another, they would make use of an encryption method. This cypher took the familiar alphabet and passed it through a secret conversion technique, supposedly making use of the Maltese Cross. Attempts to recreate this code in modern times have often been linked to freemasonry. As we will discover later in this book, attempts to uncover the code have led to many of our modern secret societies attempting to replicate, copy, or break the code without success. To this day, we have been unable to break the Templars banking cipher.

The rise from an impoverished monastic order to international bankers had not only created one of the world's first financial institutions, but it had given the Knights Templar a power beyond anything they could have expected. Less than a hundred years after their creation, they were one of the most powerful groups in Europe, if not the world. But they were still shrouded in secrecy. Only the brothers of the order were privy to their internal dealings and machinations. Their military contributions had gradually become overshadowed by their dealings in economics. While still an essential part of the military in the Holy Land, their true power came from their wealth, influence, and their holdings. With this power, they began to attract the jealous attentions of many throughout Europe. Just as quickly as they had risen to power, the Templars soon found themselves in peril.

The Downfall

In medieval Europe, just as now, it is impossible to build up such a huge amount of power and influence so quickly without attracting covetous attention from across the globe. As well as the sworn enemies of the Templars (the non-Christians), there were an increasing number of people who sought to undermine, share, and acquire the power they had so quickly accrued. In a dark time, it would be a dark process by which the enemies of the Knights Templar would wage their campaign against the order.

In addition to the banking and political influence of the Templars, it is important to remember their military prowess. Following the First Crusade, those who had been driven from the Holy Land had not simply accepted defeat. Fighting had continued, though it had ebbed and flowed in its intensity. As well as cementing their position as a banking institution, the Templars became more and more important to the Christians' armed forced. A key tenet of the Templars was the idea that they would never retreat from battle. This made them fearsome opponents. While the knights of the order fought on the front lines, many other members followed them. These members were tasked with finding anything that might benefit the order, whether that be loot or items of political importance. As the Christian army moved across the Near East, the Templars both led the line and scoured the conquered territories for anything that might help consolidate their power.

Also important was their use of tactics. It was one of their chief exponents, Bernard of Clairvaux, who had suggested that a small force could defeat a much larger one, should the conditions be right. One of the order's greatest victories was a demonstration of this theory, with the Templars lining up in 1177 against the famed Muslim leader Saladin. The ensuing Battle of Montgisard featured 26,000 Islamic warriors taking on a small band of 500 knights and their various supporting forces. Saladin had set his sights on moving north into Jerusalem and had pinned down the Christians in a small coastal town. Arriving to reinforce the Crusaders, 80 Templars met with their allies. They had initially met Saladin's forces near Gaza, but the group had been so small that the larger army had considered them too insignificant to bother dealing with. The Templars moved to join with the Crusaders while Saladin permitted his forces the opportunity to pillage some local villages. The Templars planned a surprise attack with their allies and set an ambush. They routed the Muslim army who were spread too thin to fight back, and were forced to retreat. Saladin's army fled with only ten percent of their original number, but they lived to fight another day. The battle is considered an example of the Templar's incredible military abilities and their fighting skills.

The Squadron Charge

One of the most famous tactics of the Templars embodies their commitment to their faith. A heavily armored group of knights would line up and launch what was known as a 'squadron charge', wherein they would gather themselves into a tight formation and simply charge as fast as possible at the enemy. The manner of their charge suggested that they were fully prepared to die on their arrival and would have the powerful effect of forcing a hole in the opposing ranks as the soldiers broke away from their ranks to flee the oncoming Templars.

And the Templars were not limited to using their own armies — they would be key men in almost every Christian military. They fought alongside the Kings of England and France, either leading the charge or protecting the army's most important members. Their fighting was not even limited to the Near East, as they were vital members of the war efforts in Spain and Portugal as the European Christians fought back the Muslim forces who we encroaching as part of the much-feared southerly pincer movement. They were valued members of the front line wherever Christianity fought its fiercest battles. Not only were they rich, but they were admired and trusted. These qualities engendered just as much jealousy as the wealth of the Templars.

The Knights Templar were not the only monastic order. Others, such as the Teutonic Knights and the Knights Hospitaller had arisen in similar circumstances, but were not nearly as successful. Though they worked towards ostensibly the same goals, the other orders soon grew concerned with the powers and privileges allowed to the Templars. In addition, various members of the European aristocracy noted their worries about the emerging political influence of the Knights Templar, who seemed to control an army of ever-increasing size that was not restrained by recognized borders.

The Second Crusade

One of the first stumbles came when the Templars' famed military acumen failed them. In 1187, they once again met the forces of Saladin at the Battle of the Horns of Hattin. This would later become known as a key moment in the history of the Crusades and one of the turning points in the Islamic control of the region. While they had beaten Saladin before, this time the Muslim commander was ready for the Templars. The order's leader at the time, Gerard de Ridefort, was not known as a particularly keen tactician and had only been head of the Templars for a few years. He was in command of the battle. One of his worst mistakes was venturing forth with his band of 80 knights with inadequate food, drink, and other essential supplies. Before long, the heat got to them and they were overwhelmed by Saladin's forces. The battle was a launching point for the Islamic forces. Within a few short months, they had captured Jerusalem and the main headquarters of the Templars.

This only prompted further aggression from the Christians and a renewed desire to retake the territory. Led by Richard I of England – Richard the Lionheart – a new Crusade was launched. The Templars played a key role in the military and re-established the Crusader states as they had been many years before. This time, the Templars chose to set up their headquarters in the city of Acre. Following this successful Crusade, the Templars took on even more power. The region became reliant on orders such as their own to maintain Christian control of the region. Having erected huge castles and fortifications in the area, it fell on orders such as the Templars – people who were there permanently – to guard, man, and defend these buildings. As well as their powers in the region, the Templars' land holdings reached new heights when they acquired the island of Cyprus. However, every increase in wealth and power for the Templars during this century only did more to hammer the nails into their coffin. As they gained more and more, the covetous, jealous, and worried nobility of Europe watched. By the time the end of the thirteenth century came around, people were beginning to become more and more vocal in their condemnation of the Knights Templar.

Fighting in the Near East continued. In 1244, the Christians would lose Jerusalem for the last time. A Christian nation would not rule over the city again until the British invaded during the First World War. As the Islamic world gained a stronger and stronger foothold in the region, the Templars were continually forced to relocate. They lost their homes in Acre, Tortosa, and Atlit. Eventually, they withdrew their headquarters to Cyprus, a good distance from the Holy Land and the location of all of their original goals. This, too, was lost. The Mamluks from Egypt invaded and took the final Templar foothold in the Near East.

Leaving the Holy Land

By this time, however, the Knights Templar had a presence in most major cities. Their power was spread across Europe. They had risen over the last two centuries to become an ever-present and almost essential part of day-to-day Christian life. They still owned their Templar houses, many businesses, and ran their banking empire. They held debts from a number of powerful people — people who were not pleased to be owing the Templars money. Free from the laws and taxes of any country, they were essentially a nation without land, existing wherever they had property. They even had a standing army, one which no longer had a clear military aim, now that the Holy Land had been lost. This army was free to move anywhere in Europe. In addition to this, there had been rumors that the Templars were interested in founding their own monastic country, a place of their own. Should they manage to do so, they would become one of the continent's most influential power brokers.

The death knell began to sound in 1305. Over two hundred years after the Knights Templar had been founded, their original champions within the Catholic Church had long since passed away. A new Pope reigned, one with the idea to merge the Templars with the Hospitallers. He dispatched letters to the heads of both orders broaching the possibility and was met with negative reactions from both camps. Though not as powerful as the Templars, the Hospitallers were a proud order in their own right. Eventually, persisting with the idea, Pope Clement V invited both Jacques de Molay of the Templars and Fulk de Villaret of the Hospitallers to meet him in 1306. The head of the Templars arrived first, though he did not reach the meeting point until 1307. De Villaret followed a few months later, neither party in a rush.

While waiting for the arrival of De Villaret, the Pope and De Molay discussed allegations that had been made against the Templars by a departing member. These allegations had been championed by a powerful man, King Philip IV. Philip was king of France and no friend to the Templars. Though most agreed that the allegations and rumors were false, they were damning enough that the Pope sent a letter to Philip asking for clarity. Philip had been waging a war with England and had managed to work himself deep into debt with the Templars. According to historians such as Malcolm Barber, Philip began to use the allegations to put pressure on the Church and the order, as a means of potentially freeing himself from the huge debt. Not only this, but the supposed location for the Templars new monastic state was Languedoc, in the southeast of France. There was also a religious motivation. If he was able to demonstrate the heresy of the Templars, Philip could claim his position as a defender of the Catholic faith and could cement his importance in the power structure of the Church. Should he successfully protect the Pope from the Templars' supposed influence, his role as protector would rank him above the Holy See, a move Julien Théry suggests could have led to the establishment of a holy theocracy in France.

The King of France

Before the investigation could continue, Philip pre-empted the Pope's efforts to investigate the rumors. He launched an operation to have scores of the Templars' French members arrested. They were taken away and tortured. These were not the front line, military leaders of the order, but rather those focused on the day-to-day economics of the Templars. Under torture, the members confessed to heretical tendencies, as well as other offences to God and the Church. Following their confessions, they were killed. Philip used these confessions to launch a series of charges against the entire organization of the Knights Templar. He suggested that they had:

1.   Required new recruits to spit on the cross as part of their initiation.
2.   The new recruits were then stripped and their navels, posteriors, and mouths kissed.
3.   The order told new recruits that outlawed lusts (sexual practices) were in fact natural and practiced regularly.
4.   The cords used by members to tie their robes was wrapped around a false idol and worshipped.

5.   And finally, that the members did not partake in mass.

As well as these initial charges, Philip's agents further exaggerated the crimes. The Templars were accused of worshipping a three-faced cat, denying Christ, urinating on a crucifix, and worshipping the devil. Over the coming years, nearly 140 Templars would be arrested, tortured, and often executed. The vast majority confessed to the charges, whether they were true or not. The only evidence used was the confessions of the accused. The Knights Templar desperately sought out the Pope for assistance. Despite half-heartedly sending a letter, the Pope soon simply allowed the persecutions to take place.

The resulting rumors caused a scandal. Crowds of people took to the streets to demand the blaspheming Templars be prosecuted. Pressured by both King Philip and the baying public, Pope Clement laid down the *Pastoralis Praeeminentiae*, essentially a death sentence for the order. It decreed that every monarch in Europe should arrest every Templar they could and seize every asset they could. Though many rulers did not believe the charges, they began to make arrests in Germany,

England, Italy, and other countries, including Cyprus. Whether or not the authorities could get a confession was typically dependent on whether or not the Templars were tortured.

Following the arrests, King Philip smashed the Templars' banking system. He took their wealth for himself and cancelled his own debts. As Gordon Napier notes, it is highly unlikely that he actually believed the charges to be true. Instead, he simply seized on the chance to swing the axe against the Templars and turn the balance of power in his favor. Whether there was a grain of truth in the rumors of the devil worshipping, homosexually-inclined Knights Templar, we may never know. What we do know is that, following Philip's orders, hundreds (if not thousands) of people were arrested, horribly tortured, and then executed across Europe.

Dissolution

In 1312, following further pressure from King Philip, a new Pope was convinced to officially dissolve the Knights Templar. A large amount of the order's properties were turned over to the papacy, while many of the Templars who had survived the purges were taken in by orders such as the Hospitallers. But certain elements of the order survived. In Portugal, the Templars changed their name to the Order of Christ and continued about their business. Others fled into the areas considered wilderness by the Catholic Church: Scotland, the Holy Land, and other countries where the Church's influence was not felt quite so invasively in every element of day-to-day life.

But what of the remaining Templars? At the time of the purge, the Knights Templar had over 15,000 properties across Europe and the Near East. They owned an armada of ships and an entire army. As well as the Knights and the main figures within the order, many lesser members were essential to the daily running of the Templars' economic empire. In France alone, the authorities were able to arrest 3,000 members. The Templars' archives were never recovered, having been either hidden or destroyed, despite the Pope ordering they be handed over to the Hospitallers.

From the ashes of the Knights Templar have emerged hundreds of theories. With so much wealth, property, power, and influence, that they could disappear almost overnight seems impossible. It is during this part of the tale, when we reflect on the possible alternate histories, potential futures, and dark secrets of the order that we start to see the truly fascinating elements of the Templars twisted history.

Now that we have a good overview of the history of the Knights Templar, we can start to look deeper into the secrets, mysteries, and theories surrounding their demise…and possible survival.

The Templar Fleet

One of the most popular theories about the demise of the Knights Templars combines the typical conspiracy tropes of a mysterious death, a huge fortune, and the emergence of a secret society. The theory suggests that a group of French Templars were able to escape persecution and fled to a new home. It has not only been discussed in more shrouded circles, but one of the bestselling books on the subject discusses the theory at length.

The legend tells us that the Templars had stationed 18 ships in the French harbor of La Rochelle. When the news first broke of the orders given to place them under arrest, the members of the order began to prepare for their departure. The knights gathered up treasure, documents, and important other valuables into the boats. The depths of the Templar vaults were filled not only with gold and jewels, but the tools of a true power broking society. They had paperwork relating to the various members of the order, their organization, and their structure. They possessed documents detailing their history and others listing the debts they were owed. They even possessed strange and mysterious items, relics, and assets which we can only guess at. All that can be said for sure about these vessels, however, is that they were heavy with the weight of many of the Templars greatest riches.

Just before the warrant for the arrest of every member of the order was given in 1307, the ships set sail. The evidence we have for this departure rests on the words of one man, Jean de Châlon, a member of the Templars. He told people that he had head that Gerard de Villiers had gone to sea with 18 of the Templars' galleys, while members like Hughes de Chalon had exited France with the entire treasury belonging to Hughes de Pairaud. All other utterances of these ships' departure is notably absent from history. In situations like this, we can either assume that Jean was spreading rumors, or that he was the one brother who let slip the existence of a secret exit plan. We know that the person who wrote down Jean's statement certainly took it to be simply rumor, while we also know that Jean was among those who was prone to inventing (or simply confessing) the wildest truths about the Knights Templar. Many people doubt the credibility of Jean de Châlon, while other use his words as the key point in the discussion of what happened to the Templar fleet.

Fleeing to Scotland

The story was made famous by the book, 'Holy Blood, Holy Grail.' Written by Michael Baigent, Richard Leigh, and Henry Lincoln, the book has become a cornerstone of Templar-based scholarly debates. Published in 1982, it is chiefly concerned with the bloodline of Jesus Christ and trying to map out a possible list of descendants that have survived into the modern era. The Knights Templars, they suggest, was possibly the military arm of the organization known as the Priory of Sion. Though we will delve deeper into the book's theories (and the arguments for and against its veracity) later in this book, their account of the escape of the Templar fleet is one of the best-rounded and most convincing around.

As the story is recalled in 'Holy Blood, Holy Grail,' the Templars who fled from France departed to Scotland. At the time, Scotland was fighting against the English for independence and the arrival of a small band of French monks (or so they appeared) might have escaped comment. Unlike many of the other major countries around Europe, the distractions and decentralized nature of the Scottish rebellion meant that there was not a government in place to execute the Papal orders. The man in charge of the Scottish rebellion, Robert the

Bruce, had been excommunicated from the Catholic Church at the request of the English. For the Templars, this provided them with a place they could hide out until the persecution against their order died down.

Other historians have suggested that the Templars traveled to even farther-flung corners of the Earth. In this version of events, the Templars crossed the Atlantic Ocean and found themselves in North America. The legend suggests that they arrived in Nova Scotia, in Canada, whereupon they buried their treasure at a place called Oak Island. This part of the theory has been roundly dismissed, however, by historians such as Helen Nicholson. Nicholson points out that the ships that were available to the Templars at the time would have been unsuitable for crossing as large a body of water as the Atlantic, and especially unsuitable for making a journey through previously uncharted and unknown waters. Even if there exists evidence that some Old World cultures traveled to the New World before Columbus, the idea that the Templars would have managed it is somewhat farfetched. As Michael Baigent and Richard Leigh point out, the Templar fleet was geared towards Mediterranean travel, or short trips around the area to restock companions in the Holy Land. Baigent and Leigh also note that trade with the British Isles was frequent, and that one of their primary ports for such trade was La Rochelle. Should they have wished to set sail from this part of France, Scotland was certainly a more likely destination that Canada.

A Stop in Portugal

Should the Templars have managed to escape the French prosecutors, another possible port of call was Almourol Castle, off the coast of Portugal. Unlike their Iberian neighbors, Spain and Portugal remained loyal to the Templars throughout their persecution, even hosting the Order of the Knights of Christ (an essentially re-branded branch of the Templars). This castle was representative of many of the fortifications used by the Templars, including towers and crenulations much like those found on other fortresses used and operated by the order. The Castle itself was built on the site of ancient defenses by a man named Gualdim Pais, a Master of the Knights Templar. Almourol would have provided the perfect destination for a fleet of fleeing Templars to hide for a short period, whether they were fleeing elsewhere or stopping in Portugal on a permanent basis.

According to Baigent and Leigh, the fleeing Templars made the journey from France to Almourol. Here, they met up with other members from across Europe and stayed a short while. They then fled up Ireland's west coast – where the order had a number of properties – and made the final steps of their journey across to

Scotland. They arrived at known Templar locations such as Kilmartin, Kiilmory, and Castle Sweet and began to unload their vessels. While the majority of the theories relating to the Templars are focused on the items that were unloaded in these ports – whether they were treasures, relics, or something else – Baigent and Leigh go further in their documentation of the Templars actions.

A Local Rebellion

The arrival of a band of militaristic, persecuted monastic knights in rebellious Scotland could well have shaped the course of British history. At the time, Robert the Bruce was leading his Scottish forces against the English but found himself severely outnumbered. Things came to a head in 1314, just a few years after the departing French Templars supposedly landed in Scotland. On June 24, Robert the Bruce was about to lead his 6,000 men into the Battle of Bannockburn in a field to the south of Edinburgh. He was coming up against 20,000 better equipped English soldiers. Despite the size of the respective forces, Robert emerged the victor. For Baigent and Leigh, the tide seemed to have been turned by Templar knights.

They note that the majority of scholars agree upon the idea that the Scottish army was composed chiefly of foot soldiers and that Robert was only able to count upon a handful of armed, mounted men. However, records indicate that during the course of the battle a fresh band of forces arrived to the English rear. These new knights drove the fear of God into the English soldiers, who turned and fled. While both the Scottish and English armies were exhausted on the field of battle, Baigent and Leigh note that panic swept through the English forces very suddenly and the King and his men were forced to flee the field. His troops followed and the pursuing Scottish forces were able to rout the departing men. The English abandoned everything as they fled, including not only their gold and silver, but their bags and their supplies. For Baigent and Leigh, the sheer terror instilled into the English army could only have come from one source: a small group of heavily armored Templars, leading their famous 'squadron charge.' Frightened by the arrival of such superior, fearless forces, the English immediately turned and ran, providing Robert the Bruce with a famous victory.

The idea of the arrival of the Templars on the battlefield is not so farfetched. King Edward of England was attempting to conquer Scotland and assert his control over the region. Robert the Bruce, already excommunicated by the Pope, saw this as an affront to his country and led his forces against King Edward in the name of freedom. For the Templars, however, Scotland had become a place of asylum. After fleeing the charges laid against them in France, much of Europe was still aggressively pursuing Templar influence in every corner of the continent. But Scotland was one place they were free from this persecution. It was entirely in their interests to see Robert victorious. Scotland retained her independence, while the Templars retained their temporary home away from the persecution of the rest of Europe.

The Templar fleet, while not one of the most blood-ridden or twisted examples of the Templar theories is, nevertheless, incredibly important. The idea of the fleeing Templars seeking sanctuary with all manner of treasures will form the basis for many of the theories we will examine in the coming chapters. As well as this, it is one of those rare alternative historical theories that not only has evidence to back it up from a number of sources, but serves to make a great deal of sense for all of those involved. As we read on, however, we will discover that the history of the Templars becomes a little bit more twisted.

Relics

Of all of the most enduring Templar myths, many of the most pressing and most interesting revolve around the existence of a number of historical relics. With two thousand years of history, the Christian faith has notably accrued a number of important and supposedly powerful items. These range from the Shroud of Turin (a piece of cloth supposedly bearing an imprint of Jesus's face) to the Arc of the Covenant (the storage device used to keep safe the tablets from which Moses learned of the Ten Commandments.)

Throughout history, the Templars have been linked to numerous relics and various items of historic importance. While not all are as feasible as the others, the multitude and regularity of the rumors indicate the suspicion with which many people treat the Knights Templar. Of all the places to start, however, it might be best to begin with their very first home, the Temple of Solomon.

The Temple of Solomon

Temple Mount is a hugely important religious site in at least four religions. Found in Jerusalem, it has been used by Paganism, Judaism, Islam, and Christianity as a place of worship. As well as traditional temples, the site has also supposedly been home to many events of religious importance. For the Jewish faith, it is traditionally the holiest place in the world. It was where God swept together dust to make Adam and was the site of the story of the binding of Isaac. This was why it was chosen by the Jewish King Solomon as a site for his temple. Thought to be the wisest man of his age, he is a figure in all three Abrahamic religions. The temple is built on top of the Foundation Stone, a rock found right at the heart of the building's base. The rock has a tiny hole in one of its corners which enters into a larger cavern located beneath the stone. This cavern is known as the Well of Souls and it is thought to be the place on Earth closest to Heaven. As well as these traditionally Jewish tales, the stories have been passed down through Islam and Christianity and the site is also hugely significant in these religions because of this.

After the First Crusade swept through Jerusalem, Temple Mount was one of the most fiercely defended sites. As both Jews and Muslims attempted to stop the Christian Crusaders gaining entry, they were cut down. According to sources at the time, the bloodstains went up to the knees of the Crusaders. But after the fighting had died down, a new order of knights found themselves in need of a home. The knights were given a wing in the Temple and took their name from the building, becoming the Knights Templar. But rather than a simple home and a nice story for the naming of a band of monastic knights, the significance of Temple Mount could be greater than anyone was prepared to admit.

The Templars were based in their original home for 75 years. For many researchers, however, the first nine years of their residence in this building seem to be the most interesting. During this time, the order's activities were incredibly clandestine. After appearing in paperwork and documentation at their founding, the discussions of the order seemed to vanish for nine years. The group's activities during this time are hotly disputed. For some, these nascent years were the source of all of the group's power. Having been given the Temple of Solomon as a base of operations, the legend goes, the Templars set out to discover more about their home. While their activity was seemingly limited to outsiders, inside they were working furiously.

Some scholars have suggested that the Templars discovered items of historical importance on the site. It is not unlikely that there was something of archaeological value to be found on Temple Mount. Even before Solomon had founded his temple on the site, it had been home to numerous buildings and its importance to Judaism had been noted. Returning to the book, 'Holy Blood, Holy Grail,' the suggestion has been that the Templars excavated the site and were able to find documents that had been hidden long before their arrival. These documents – whatever they contained – provided the Templars with enough power and influence to expand their order across Europe. Rather than being a beneficial set of lucky circumstances, the Templars' rise to power – their papal decrees and accumulation of wealth – related to the information that was contained within these words.

Indeed, the idea that the Templars discovered something beneath the base of their headquarters is key to almost every theory and mystery. Whatever it was that they found during those nine years, it was likely the same thing they hid away when they fled La Rochelle centuries later. The idea that a relic was recovered by the Templars is supported by a small amount of evidence. Piers Paul Read notes that some Templar knights were known to carry a piece of the True Cross (the one on which Jesus was crucified) into battle. However, Read also notes that this particular relic likely came from an earlier piece dating back to Saint Helena in the 4th century. If we are to uncover the truth about the Knights Templar and their powerful order, we will need to know (or at least, construct an educated guess) as to what exactly they were able to recover from the grounds of one of the holiest places in all of the world. With so many distinct possibilities, and with the order so shrouded in secrecy, the quest to discover the truth behind the Templars' power has been an obsession for many, many people.

The Copper Scroll

Another item purportedly found beneath the temple is known as the Copper Scroll. Not as famous as many of the other relics we will come across, it certainly fits well into the story of the rise of the Templars. The Copper Scroll is part of the ancient collection of writings known as the Dead Sea Scrolls. But while the other texts in the collection are literary works and shed light on the early days of Christianity, the Copper Scroll is very different.

For a start, it is not written on the papyrus or paper used by the other scrolls. Instead, its writing is carved directly into a slab of metal, specifically copper, with a tiny amount of tin. Most importantly, however, it is not a piece of literature. Instead, it is simply a list, describing the burial locations of various amounts of gold, silver, and other treasures.

Our modern knowledge of the Copper Scroll comes from its rediscovery in 1952 by a British scholar. It was the last of the collection of scrolls to be discovered and researchers believe that it was a later addition, added separately from the main bulk of the collection. The same researchers have attempted to discern the origins of the treasure. Suggestions have ranged from it being the treasure of the Temple of the Mount, before one of the numerous occasions on which it was destroyed, right up to the idea that the tablet itself is a hoax and a distraction.

Robert Eisenman has written at length about the Copper Scroll and has argued for its authenticity. He claims that the Templars actually found a duplicate of the piece during their excavations. They traveled across the Holy Land during the first nine years of their existence and tracked down the buried gold and silver. This was then used to fund their order and to begin their banking empire. This would explain the Templars quick rise to power, their huge wealth, and the fact that very few of the locations listed on the scroll have proved to be profitable when treasure hunters have gone searching.

The Copper Scroll itself is now on display in a museum in Jordan. If it was indeed a treasure map detailing the means to find the treasures of Solomon's temple, then not only is it potentially one of the most credible Templar legends, but it could also have been the key to the Templars discovering other relics scattered across the Holy Land.

The Turin Shroud

Like the Copper Scroll, the Turin Shroud (or the Shroud of Turin) is a relic that still exists to this day and is very occasionally shown to the public. However, it was not always owned by the same people. For long passages of its life, the Shroud has been out of the public's eye. It currently resides (as the name suggests) in Turin, Italy.

Despite being a simple piece of ancient linen, the relic gains its power from supposedly being the cloth which was used to wrap the body of Jesus Christ before he was first buried. When opened up, the Shroud displays the faint outlines of a man, including a vague image of a face. If it is real, then the Shroud is the closest we might ever get to looking upon the face of Jesus.

Scientists have attempted to use carbon dating methods to determine the age of the linen. Their findings seemed to suggest that the cloth came from the medieval period. While this might render the relic's holy status as negative, it does little to disassociate the Shroud's history from the Templars. Even if it were a fake, it was a fake good enough to fool people for almost 1,000 years. Should a group have the burial cloth of Jesus, they would hold a powerful relic. If it were a forgery, the very fact that people believed it to be authentic renders it almost as powerful.

The Turin Shroud's link to the Templar Knights begins around the time it was first shown to the public, in 1357. It was displayed by the widow of a recently deceased nobleman named Geoffrey of Charney. Geoffrey had supposedly inherited the Shroud from a family member. He could trace his lineage back to Geoffroi de Charney, one of the men who was executed by the French for his involvement with the Templars. Geoffroi has been one of the men burned at the stake after being tortured for a confession, placed alongside the highest ranking members of the order during his final moments.

But in 2009, paperwork emerged from the Vatican's Secret Archives which solidified the bond between the Charney family and the Shroud. Barbara Frale, a researcher, claimed to have found information which indicated that the Shroud had fallen into the possession of the Templars in 1204, alongside a collection of writings believed to be Jesus's 'burial certificate.' These writings were spread across pieces of a broken tablet, written in Greek, Hebrew, and Latin. The imprints of the words can still be seen on the Shroud.

Another recent piece of evidence linking the Shroud with the Templars is the painting found in a church in England during the 1940s. A woman named Molly Drew was searching through a home in Templecombe when she came across a picture depicting a man (either Jesus or John the Baptist) and it contains a copy of the image found on the Shroud of Turin. It is though that the Templars commissioned the painting while still in possession of the Shroud and hid it during their persecution. The painting has been carbon dated to 1280, and it is an indication of the importance the Templars placed on the Shroud, commissioning paintings to celebrate its importance and to reflect its images of Jesus.

Whether the Turin Shroud is real or not is almost irrelevant in this discussion. That the Templars almost certainly controlled one of the most important relics in Christendom is a reflection of the position of power they held within the Church. Alternatively, the idea that the Shroud is a fake just demonstrates the length to which the Templars would go to consolidate their influence and

- due to the seeming high quality of the forgery —
demonstrates the skills they possessed at the time of its
creation. Whether fake or real, we know that the
Templars possessed the Shroud of Turin for many
centuries and were able to use its power for their own
purposes.

The Ark of the Covenant

One of the stranger suggestions regarding relics the Templars might possibly have recovered relates to one of the oldest Jewish treasures. The Ark of the Covenant is the name given to the wooden box which was used to carry the stone tablets bearing the Ten Commandments Moses had received from God, as well as other items such as the Rod of Aaron and a pot of the food from heaven, Manna. The chest was used during the exodus from Egypt to preserve the words of God and was lost over the ensuing centuries.

The historian Graham Hancock wrote a book titled 'The Sign and the Seal,' in which he put forward the idea that the Templars had uncovered information at the site of Temple Mount that pointed them towards the real resting place of the Ark. While it had formerly been at the site, it was moved before the first destruction of a temple on the grounds. The priests hid the Ark in Ethiopia and the fact that the Templars knew this is acknowledged in some of the art and architecture they left. One of the best examples is the Cathedral found in Chartes, which was overseen by Bernard of Clairvaux, one of the order's greatest evangelists.

As well as discovering the resting place of the Ark, Hancock suggests that the Templars found many ancient secrets on the grounds of the temple. These secrets were not simply Church teachings or literature, but trade methods and building techniques that the Templars used in the construction of the forts and castles they built during their two centuries in power. While it is acknowledged that the discovery of the actual Ark of the Covenant is unlikely, the discussions and collection of ancient Jewish wisdom – colloquially referred to as the Ark - they might have found at Temple Mount is certainly a reasonable hypothesis. They then took this knowledge and used it to bolster their construction techniques and to build some of the most enduring and amazing fortifications seen at the time.

Before the idea is dismissed so readily, it might be worth looking to the sites that were left behind in Ethiopia. The Church of Saint George in the country was built during the medieval period and has been suggested by some scholars as being a Templar tribute to the information they uncovered in Jerusalem. While they might not have found the actual Ark, the knowledge they uncovered at the time transformed the order into the force it was destined to become.

Throughout their history, the Knights Templar have been linked with many of the relics commonly found throughout the history of Christianity. The items we have listed above are those with the best links to the order. These relics have allegedly been passed down from generation to generation, from the height of the Templars' power to the depths of their secrecy. And the secrecy plays a huge role in the story of the Knights Templar. Because they were driven from the public's eye and essentially outlawed, they have existed on the periphery of the cultural consciousness for the past six centuries. Any surviving members of the order have been happy to indulge in the rumors and theories attributed to the Templars. Because nothing can be denied, nothing can be confirmed. The Templars have been able to cloak themselves in the very rumors, secrets, and assumptions that so many people project on to them. In doing so, their true purposes are obfuscated. Despite this, there are links and rumors which carry a little bit more credence than others. In the following chapters we will examine those theories and ideas that just will not leave the Templars. For those wishing to know the truth behind the order, the following chapters contain some of the most important knowledge we have been able to pick apart from the lies, allegations, and mistruths surrounding one of history's most secret societies.

The Holy Grail

The Holy Grail is the most important relic in Christian mythology. Legend tells us that the Grail is a receptacle – a cup, a plate, a dish, or something similar- that is forever linked to the death of Christ. According to the stories, the Grail is imbued with great power and those who drink from it can receive eternal youth, everlasting contentment, and it can even heal mortal wounds. The Grail was supposedly the very same item as the one used by Jesus during the last supper. Following the crucifixion, Joseph of Arimathea took the Grail and used it to collect the blood from Christ as he hung on the cross, punctured by a Roman spear. After the death and the resurrection, the Grail was handed down from generation to generation, kept hidden and safe. For some people, the Templars were the order entrusted to defend the Grail.

The earliest mentions we can trace of the Holy Grail come from medieval French writings. The word 'graal' is used, ostensibly descended from the Latin word 'gradalis' and working its way back through Greek and Aramaic. The first descriptions seem to come from Chrétien de Troyes, who talks about the item as though it was a dish or some type of bowl. Similarly, Hélinand of

Froidmont's descriptions seem to talk about an item something like a saucer. Other writers from across Europe talked about the Grail as an item of tableware and even as a stone, but the references emerge not just from France, but from Spain, Wales, and Germany. The Holy Grail became a consistent figure in many romance stories of the medieval period, with the bravest of knights either trusted with the Grail itself or charged with hunting for it. Only the greatest and most honorable were said to be permitted to care for this most holy of relics.

Needless to say, the fame and popularity of the Grail legend emerged during the 12th and 13th centuries, the time when the Templars were rising to power. One theory put forth is that, having discovered the Grail, the order themselves spread the legend through Europe as they themselves established chapter after chapter in the various states and countries. Just as the Templars spread out from their original base atop the Temple Mount, the stories about the Holy Grail went with them. As the Templars became a regular fixture of contemporary medieval life, then the Grail became an increasingly common feature in literature and folklore. Whether this stems from the members of the order recounting tales or simply rumors spread by those who wished to know more about the Templars, all we know is that the stories of the Holy Grail have become inextricably linked to the tales of the Knights Templar.

Just as the Templars shot to fame suddenly, however, they became wanted just as quickly. If they did indeed possess the Grail, not only would it give both the Catholic Church and powerful aristocrats a reason to covet their power beyond their political influence, but it would suggest that the protection of the Grail soon became the Templars' chief mission. Though they had been founded in order to protect the Holy Land and to ensure the safe passages of pilgrims who wanted to visit Christianity's most sacred sites, they found themselves in possession of an item of far greater religious worth. Just as their attentions moved further and further away from the Holy Land, their focus turned elsewhere. With the Grail in hand, they would have had a far greater mission and one of the world's foremost links to the divine.

But as the Templars fled from the port in La Rochelle, the mission to keep the Grail safe took on new significance. While they had previously been a decentralized, militaristic order with special privileges from the Pope, they were now wanted men. In order to protect the Grail properly, they would need to go into hiding. For all the discussion about the size and importance of the Knights Templar at the time of their persecution, the relative speed with which they vanished from the face of the Earth was impressive. Should they have had something to hide – such as the holiest of relics – then they would have had good reason for taking their order underground and fleeing from the watching gazes of those who might seek to take the Grail from them.

But what exactly happened to the Holy Grail once the Templars realized that they would need to take it into hiding? We turn, once again, to our main source on the matter, 'Holy Blood, Holy Grail,' in which the authors discuss the likeliest destinations following the turning of political opinion against the order. The authors suggest that the Grail's protection was the chief concern of the Templars. In order to best protect their treasure, the Templars took it to one of two places. It is either buried beneath a small church in Scotland named the Roslyn Chapel, or it was scurried away to be hidden in Northern Spain and the current location is not known. All attempts to dig beneath the Scottish chapel have been rebuffed and, following the emergence of the Templar and Grail theory, it has become a popular tourist spot among those looking for clues as to the final resting place of the Holy Grail.

But the authors of 'Holy Blood, Holy Grail' do not suggest that the theory behind the Templar involvement with the Grail is so simple. Instead, they put forward a far more complex and twisted suggestion. Rather than being an order of knights who discovered the Grail by chance, the authors trace the existence of the Templars back even further. To truly understand their theory, we must travel back to the time of Jesus.

As discussed in 'Holy Blood, Holy Grail,' Jesus was a married man. He took a wife. Though it is not discussed in the accounts that would eventually form the Bible, one of Jesus's companions – the woman named Mary Magdalene – could in fact trace her lineage back to the ancient Jewish King David. Jesus and Mary were married, and they had children. While the biblical figure of Jesus Christ may have died at the age of 33 and left behind only his followers, the authors point to gospels not included in the Bible (known as the Apocrypha) as being evidence for the existence of a bountiful marriage between Jesus and Mary Magdalene.

From Jesus and Mary Magdalene, the descendants of the marriage continued to survive throughout the rise of Christianity. These descendants became known as scions. Though few records exist that can trace the lineage directly, it is said that hundreds of years of survival lead to the scions forming the foundation for the great French house, the Merovingian family. This group controlled the kingdom of the Franks from as early as 457 (when our records of their lineage begin) until 751, when they were overthrown. But by this time, their presence among the aristocracy of Europe was enough that their activities, births, deaths, and descendants were monitored by those who remained aware of their true identity as the scions of Christ. In order to protect them, a secret society was formed. Rather than the Knights Templar, this society was known by the name the Priory of Sion.

The Priory were sworn to secrecy and took it upon themselves to recruit only the most intelligent and trustworthy members. But as the importance of their task grew and grew, it became clear that they would need a more functional organization in order to better provide protection for the Merovingian family and their descendants. This is where the Knights Templar came in. Formed as the Priory's military and financial branch, they were charged with creating the infrastructure and military capabilities that might be needed in order to battle against anyone who might seek to destroy the scions.

But who would want to wish harm on the descendants of Jesus Christ? According to the book, one of the chief ill-wishers of the scions is the Catholic Church. Following the efforts of Saint Paul to establish the first Church and to spread the word of God around the world via Catholicism, the institution had become one of the most powerful in the world and, more importantly, the line of Popes became the chief religious authority among men. Should the real identity of the scions ever be revealed, they would pose a threat to the power wielded by the papacy. Similarly, the Merovingian family still retained a certain amount of aristocratic respect and influence among the French population and nobility. At a time when a war of succession could see dynasties rise and fall, the ruling French kings were not entirely pleased that the traditional rulers of the country might be lurking around in the shadows, especially if they had a supposedly divine right to rule. It was a combination of these two bodies – King Philip and the Pope – who broke apart the Priory's most visible wing, the Knights Templar.

In response to this attack, the Templars reverted to the behavior of the more secretive Priory of Sion. They went into hiding. Their members simply stepped back from public view and those most in control of the true intentions of the order were able to operate far from the prying eyes of their prosecutors. The Priory went on to include very famous men as members. Among the most notable were Leonardo da Vinci and Isaac Newton, who at various times throughout the Renaissance and Enlightenment headed up the Priory in the position of Grand Master (the same title as the head of the Templars.) They operated under the very noses of the Church and the aristocratic families who might seek to damage, attack, or otherwise harm the descendants of Jesus.

But what evidence exists for the idea that the Holy Grail was in fact a royal lineage, rather than a special cup? One of the most pressing discussed by the authors of 'Holy Blood, Holy Grail' is the one theory which gives the book its title. When looking through the early literary interpretations of the Holy Grail – those which did the most work to define the modern conception of the Grail as a cup – we must look to the old French sources. Here, we find a possible error, confusion, or intentional mistranslation. The name in Old French for the Holy

Grail is 'san graal' or 'san gréal.' But if one letter in these words were to move, the meaning changes entirely. Move the letter 'g' and change the phrase from 'san greal' to 'sang real' and the translation is altered significantly. 'Sang real' translates to 'royal blood,' and with that alteration comes the idea that the Templars were not trying to protect a holy item, but the royal blood line itself. What the Templars found buried beneath the Temple of Solomon might have been the lineage of the scions, tracing the history of the Jewish prophet Jesus Christ into the medieval period and the truth about the descendants of Christ. This would then bolster the proof the Priory had of the history of the scions, as well as provide a huge amount of powerful documents that the Templars would need to rush away to a hiding place as soon as they were placed under arrest. When fleeing, it could well have been these ancient family trees that the Templars were taking with them, hiding the existence of the scions away from the marauding forces of the French King and the Catholic Church.

The idea of the Grail being a bloodline is not as farfetched as you might think. It is not uncommon for the royal families of Europe to be able to trace their lineage back hundreds and even thousands of years. In the case of the Merovingian dynasty, they were one of the most powerful families around, and were supposedly descended from a clan of Israelites or people of Middle Eastern origin. In combining this history with the speculative, it is not impossible that they are able to trace their history back over many hundreds of years before they rose to power in the 8th century.

The theory does not even preclude a religious element. The historicity of Jesus Christ has been debated for many years. Aside from the divine aspect of his legend, whether he was an actual historical figure – a real man – is less questioned. If we are to believe biblical historians such as Robin Fox, Richard Carrier, and John Dickson, then the fact that a man named Jesus existed around the time of 2BC to 30BC is agreed upon with a "near universal consensus." The accuracy of the biblical accounts, the gospels, the teachings of the Catholic Church, and the belief of individuals in situations such as these is almost irrelevant. Instead, our information comes from apocryphal texts from the time, primary sources that were not created with any specific religious intent (as might be found in the bible.) Roman sources such as Tacitus and Jewish sources such as Josephus give us a non-Christian perspective on the man. But they are in agreement: Jesus of Nazareth was a real man.

If we are to accept this thesis – that there lived a Jewish man named Jesus during the early years of the 1st millennium who built up a cult following before being executed – then we can speculate on the likelihood of his having fathered children. It was extremely common, practically expected, that a man would be married before the time he reached thirty. In fact, were it not the case during this time period, then this fact would have been commented on by the people who wrote about Jesus's life. That his family is rarely mentioned either means that there was no family (something very irregular for the time period) or that it was mundane enough not to draw notice. Following this trail of thought, the idea that he might have birthed a dynasty is not irreconcilable. From there, the idea of the Templars safeguarding the very records of this bloodline accounts for their sudden rise to power, their considerable influence, the anger which they elicited in some of the most powerful people, and their willingness to vanish back into the shadows.

While it might seem the more outlandish of the two suggestions, the idea that the Holy Grail is a dynasty rather than a magic cup is actually a far more reasonable suggestion. One does not even need to presume that Jesus of Nazareth was anything more than a preacher in the Holy Land who happened to be killed by the Romans in a particularly gruesome fashion. The divinity of the man does not dictate the possibility that he left behind a family. That he became so important following his death simply deepened the possibility that people would feel the need to document his descendants. The Templars, should this theory be true, form a small part of a wider picture. If you would like to dig deeper into the history of the Priory of Sion and the influence they have had on the world, there is a further reading section at the end of this book. For now though, we will move on to other theories put forward which threaten to shed light on the dark past of the Knights Templar.

De Molay's Curse

As fascinating as the rise and fall of the Knights Templar can be, one of the most important moments came right on the precipice between the moment when they were most powerful and the moment when they became outlaws. At this time, the brutality and bloodlust enjoyed by their enemies was almost unmatched in its prejudice. Not until the Protestant Reformation would Christian Europe encounter such a violent schism. Amid the executions, one man unleashed a curse upon his oppressors. It is only with hindsight that we can witness the scale and the scope of the curse of Jacques de Molay. But who was he, and why did his death cause such violent resonations?

We know little of Jacques' early years. It is reasonable to assume that he was born into a well-to-do family in the region of Burgundy, in modern day France. At the time, it was under the control of the Holy Roman Empire and ruled by Otto III. We know that he was born sometime between 1240 and 1250, though the exact year eludes us. As with many men who would eventually rise high in the ranks of the Templars, he was part of the nobility. This afforded him the chance to train as a knight and, when he was close to twenty years old, this training was rewarded with an invitation to join the order of the Knights Templar. Over the ensuing decades, he did work on behalf of the Templars, moving between France and the Holy Land.

In 1291, the Templar base in Acre fell to the invasion of the Mamluks from Egypt. De Molay was part of the forces who managed to escape with much of their wealth to set up their headquarters on the island of Cyprus. Here, Jacques de Molay was stationed with the most important man in the order, Thibaud Gaudin, the twenty-second Grand Master. In 1292, Gaudin died and the order was left with little in the way of legitimate contenders to take over the role. De Molay, despite his relative lack of experience, put himself forward. He made it his mission to rekindle interest in taking the Holy Land back in the name of Christendom and used this pretext to tour around the capitals of Europe, seemingly to raise support. He found it tough to secure any firm promises of forces from the ruling classes, with few wanting to commit to a new Crusade. He was faced with papal requests that he merge the order with the Knights Hospitaller. Faced with the threat of the Egyptian Mamluks attacking Cyprus, he even tried to forge an alliance with a Mongol army in the East to sweep through Syria and remove the Islamic rulers in the region. This proposed alliance with the Mongols would have caught the Holy Land in a pincer movement between the Templars and the Mongols. But the Mongols never arrived. Despite the promise of helping the Crusaders and Templars in 1300, 1301, and 1302, the promised army never showed. De Molay watched on as the Crusaders lost their last footholds in the Holy Land and saw the Mamluks take over the island of Cyprus.

Jacques de Molay and his Knights Templar retreated to Europe. As we have discussed earlier in the book, Pope Clement V and King Philip IV began to place the order under increased amounts of pressure. King Philip's influence over the Catholic Church at this point was certainly dubious. Recognizing the French king's intentions, Pope Boniface VIII (one of Clement's predecessors) had attempted to have Philip excommunicated. Instead, Boniface was kidnapped and charged with committing heresy. The ordeal caused the elderly Pope to die of shock. He was followed by Pope Benedict XI, who died less than a year after taking charge in Rome. According to Helen Nicholson, it is quite likely that one of Philip's close friends, Guillaume de Nogaret, poisoned the Pope. Finally, when Clement took charge of the Church, he immediately recognized Philip's power, even moving the headquarters of Catholicism to Poitiers, in France. This was where Jacques de Molay arrived, unaware of the undue influence the King of France had over the papacy, and hoping to save his order from persecution.

As we know, he failed. Charges of heresy were lodged against the Knights Templar and orders issued for their arrest. Jacques de Molay was in Paris on the 12th of October, having attended the funeral of Catherine of Courtenay, the sister-in-law of the French King. He had carried her coffin from the church to the grave, a very great honor and one for which he had been specifically requested. The very next day, at dawn, he and his Templars were arrested by the King's men. The allegations were remarkably similar to those pressed against Pope Boniface VIII when Philip had accused him of heresy. In the political game of cat and mouse, King Philip had cornered the Grand Master of the Knights Templar.

Jacques de Molay was taken to the University of Paris. Over the course of two days (the 24th and 25th of October,) he was repeatedly tortured by Philip's guardsmen. After 48 hours of torture, he was ready to admit that the Templars had, among other things, denied Jesus Christ and stamped on the cross. He signed a letter admitting to such actions and this letter was used by the King to force Pope Clement V to issue an arrest for the Knights Templar in every Christian nation.

But Clement was still not satisfied. He was unsure of the legitimacy of the confession and – behind Philip's back – he sent a pair of his trusted cardinals to talk to De Molay. They arrived in December and began to talk to the Grand Master, who took back everything he had confessed. For the next six months, the Pope stood up to Philip as they argued over how best to handle the Templar situation. It was agreed that the Knights Templar would be investigated by two bodies, one who would judge the individual members and one who would judge the order in its entirety.

Jacques de Molay, Grand Master of the Knights Templar, remained under lock and key. As the King of France and the Pope struggled for control of the persecution of the Knights Templar, he was occasionally wheeled out from his cell to appear before various courts. Sometimes he admitted to the crimes he was accused of, while other times he recanted his confessions. Appearing bedraggled, in pain, but still defiant, De Molay refused to go gently into the night. This infuriated King Philip so much that he simply decided, one day, to use the forced confessions as the one piece of evidence he needed. Despite the findings of various courts, despite the fact that the confessions had been withdrawn, and despite the hideous torture which the men had been placed under, King Philip sentenced De Molay and 53 other members of the Knights Templar to be burned at the stake.

Our best account of the morning of the death of Jacques de Molay comes from Henry Charles Lea, who was present. As he tells us, a scaffold platform was erected outside of the famous Notre Dame Cathedral. Jacques de Molay was wheeled out before the crowds. As the Grand Master, he was one of the more recognizable Templars, but many other high-ranking order members were there as well. It had been nearly seven years since the group had been arrested, and they had languished in a jail cell for the entire time. Members of the clergy were brought out to add authority to the judgement that was about to pass.

Because the Templars had been accused of such sordid crimes, they were facing a gruesome death. But before they could be executed, both Jacques de Molay and Geoffroi de Charney stood to address the crowd. Speaking in public for the first time in years, the men insisted upon their innocence. Their real crime was their lack of loyalty to the order of the Knights Templar and they were indeed guilty of betraying their vows, rather than the heresy with which they were charged. The charges, they insisted, were false, as were the confessions. The members of the clergy were perturbed by this turn of events and didn't know what to do. When King Philip discovered the executions had been delayed, he was apoplectic. He ruled that, regardless of their words, the Templars were heretics and were to be burned at the stake. The men were taken to the lle des Juifs, an island on the Siene which is close to the grounds of the palace. Here, the Templars were burned alive. They died slowly but refused any help that was offered to them. Henry Charles Lea commends the dignity and composure with which the Templars died and notes that their martyr status was confirmed by the people in attendance, who collected the ashes from the fire and claimed them as relics.

But the death was not quite so simple. As he stood in the fires, the flames licking up around his bare flesh and blistering his skin, Jacques de Molay lashed out with his tongue. As he died his slow and painful death, with the nerves endings in his skin roasting one by one, De Molay screamed out a curse on his persecutors. Philip IV and Clement V, he bellowed, would soon join him. Before the end of the year, they too would be standing in front of God to answer for what they had done. As the smoke and the flames rose higher and higher, those in attendance heard the curse, but could not know just how unerringly accurate it would become.

King Philip's death was entirely unexpected. At the age of 46, several months after the executions of the Templars, he took to one of his beloved hunting trips. Though he was a relatively healthy man and surrounded by attendants, they could do nothing to prevent their King being struck down by a stroke. After the initial attacks, Philip spent the next few weeks attempting to recover from this accident and surviving in great pain. He died shortly after.

Pope Clement's death was even stranger. Despite his age, his death was equally unexpected. After being discovered dead, his body was laid in state as is tradition. Over the church, however, a huge thunderstorm began to brew. In the deepest darkness of the night, a lightning bolt struck the church where his body was kept and set it ablaze. The church burned so fiercely and the flames were so hot that, despite the rain and people's attempts to quell the fire, the building was destroyed. With it, Clement's body was damaged beyond all recognition. After less than a year, Jacques de Molay's curse had been fulfilled.

Our account of the curse comes from a man who was present at the burning of the Templars. Geoffrey of Paris was the man who recorded the curse, which was discovered by Malcolm Barber. The stories of the curse have also been passed down elsewhere, however, and ancient rituals involving the Freemasons (whom we will cover in the next chapter) have demanded that those welcomed into the order trample on a papal tiara and a French crown, enacting vengeance on behalf of De Molay. The scars of his death have been remembered by this organization with close ties to the Templars.

The final chapter in the history of the curse of De Molay comes during another turbulent time in France's history.

During the French Revolution, King Louis XVI of France was executed. He was taken to the guillotine and beheaded in public in 1793. Legend says that nearly five hundred years after a French King had publically executed the Grand Master of the Templars, a man ran from the crowd in the square before the guillotine. According to whomever you choose to believe, he either thrust his hand into the pool of royal blood or lifted the severed head up to the crowd. As he did so, he screamed to the watching people, "Jacques de Molay, you have been avenged!"

The Freemasons

Any discussion of a secret society will eventually come round to the Freemasons. The Knights Templar are no different and – over the course of the last 800 years – people have tried to link the monastic order to Freemasonry on many occasions. While the Freemasons are a dark and mysterious institution in their own right, their links to the Templars are built on far more solid foundations than you might expect.

As with many theories about the Templars, the chief area of interest with regards to Freemasonry only begins once the Templars were forced into hiding. The fleet of Templar vessels that departed from La Rochelle is again the origin of the theory, with people choosing to accept the standard theory that the Templars relocated to Scotland in order to freely go about their business. The ties to the Freemasons begin once the Templars land in Scotland.

Thanks to our knowledge of some of the secret rituals of the Freemasons, we know that references to the Templars exist within their bylaws. The Ancient and Accepted Scottish Rite contains degrees such as the

Knight of Rose-Croix (the Rose Cross) and the Knight of Saint Andrew, both of which contain bylaw references to the Templars. In fact, the Freemason's 32nd Degree in Consistory makes a direct reference to the Masonic Knights Templar, but some have tried to dismiss these references as being purely ceremonial, rather than historical.

Others, such as John Robinson, have suggested that the bond runs much deeper than mere mentions in rule books. In his book, 'Born in Blood,' Robinson delves into the secrets he has uncovered about freemasonry. He agrees with the theory that the Templars fled to Scotland in the 1300s in order to escape the wrath of the French king and the Catholic Church. The members of the order beseeched the locals for sanctuary. They finally found refuge with a lodge run by the local Scottish masons who specialized in stonework. Staying with the lodge, the Templars began to impart their chivalric values and religious beliefs. In order to teach the stonemasons about these qualities, they made use of the tools and items they found around the lodge, using them as metaphors for their lessons, establishing what would become the discourse of Freemasonry.

In no time, the lodge and the Templars expanded their group to include outsiders and people from the surrounding areas. These were called 'speculative masons' and their presence was seen by the Templars as a means of continuing their teachings in the less-than-ideal political climate. If the Knights Templar were to be driven into the ground, then this new group would be able to stand for many of the same values they had once embodied. This practice laid the foundations for a clandestine society who continued to remain in the shadows for the next several centuries, eventually revealing themselves in 1717 and taking on the name, 'The United Grand Lodge of England.'

One of their greatest treasures has already been mentioned in this text. The Rosslyn Chapel, found in Scotland, is unique in its architecture. Anyone who walks into the church will immediately notice the idiosyncratic decorations. Rather than conventional Christian imagery, the church is covered in symbols, logos, designs, and characters from across the world. It is not limited to Christianity, but also includes Islamic, Hindi, Nordic, Celtic, Pagan, and many, many other cultural artifacts. The Earls of Rosslyn, who ordered the construction of the chapel, have long held ties to Freemasonry and are believed to have been directly involved in the creation of the church. Despite the fact that the chapel was created 100 years after the initial purge of the Templars, it not only encapsulates the teaching of both the Freemasons and the Templars, but is a physical manifestation of the close ideological links between the two organizations. This point is also made by Michael Baigent and Richard Leigh in their book, 'The Temple and the Lodge.'

Even if the links between the Knights Templar and the Freemasons are hard to prove, why does it matter? Beyond the general conspiracy theories involving the Freemasons and their influence on world culture, the idea that one of the world's foremost secret societies could so heavily influence another is fascinating. Perhaps more interestingly, the Freemasons have managed to achieve a level of cultural acceptance that the Templars never managed. Aside from fringe criticism, Masonic presence is noted in almost every major city in the world and, typically, this passes without comment or concern. Unlike the Templars, whose presence and influence was unnerving for many major political powers, the Freemasons have managed to position themselves within society where they are essentially accepted.

With this in mind, the idea of the Templars directly influencing the birth of the Freemasons means that they were able to preserve many of their ideals and principals. In essence, the Templar influence on a second secret society allowed them to reinvent their order as something more socially accepted. In the 14th century, with the Crusades long over and no need for a militaristic presence in the Holy Land, as well as a growing list of enemies, the Knights Templar were in trouble. When this reached a head and they were forced to flee France, the Templars came up with a new solution. They reinvented themselves. Allying with a different society altogether, they were able to create a new order in an image better suited to contemporary society. They were able to use everything they had learned and impart everything they held dear, passing it on to the nascent Freemasons. Rather than a fighting religious order, this new society was a profession-oriented secret group. On the surface, they may have differed from the Freemasons, but deep down, the Templars were able to preserve their qualities and ensure they survived for generations to come.

The further removed we get from the initial contact between the Templars and the Freemasons, the more difficult it becomes to gather concrete information about their shared practices. While the Templars have fallen away into rumor, myth, and legend, the Freemasons have thrived. The handing of the baton between these secret societies could well have contained far more than simply codes of honor and chivalric practices. Instead, the secrets of the Templars may have been buried deep inside the core foundations of the Freemasons. Whether that relates to the truth about the Holy Grail, lingering prejudices involving the curse of Jacques de Molay, or just an incredible amount of wealth and treasure, we can only speculate.

Legacy

Having existed for close to nine hundred years, the Knights Templar have left a series of marks on our cultural landscape. Their presence and influence can be noticed in everything from their widespread logo — the red cross emblazoned across the white background — right down to the structure of the modern banking systems around the world. But there are many, many ways in which the Templars have left their mark, and some which you might never have imagined.

One popular legend connects the Knights Templar to the superstition surrounding the date Friday the 13th. In many Western cultures, this occasional arrangement of the date is considered to an unfortunate day, with bad experiences and poor luck often attributed to the day itself. It's held in the superstitions in much the same way as people might treat a black cat crossing their path or walking beneath a ladder. The legend goes back to Friday, October the 13th, 1307, the day on which the order for the arrest of every Templar knight was carried out. With these knights and order members then tortured and executed on the order of King Philip, the date became closely associated with the death of the

Templars. Over the coming centuries, the times when the 13th of the month coincided with a Friday became engrained in superstition and the demise of the Templars.

Another commonly overlooked legacy of the Templars is the architectural treasures they left behind. With this presence stretching from the Holy Land to the furthest tips of Europe, they developed a reputation as master builders. Among the fortifications they left behind are:

- Sidon Sea Castle in Lebanon
- Commandry of Coulommiers, France
- Chastel Blanc, Syria
- Château Pèlerin, Israel
- San Bevignate church, Italy
- Castle of Almourol, Portugal
- Tourbillon Castle, Sion, Switzerland
- Tempelhof, Berlin, Germany
- The Temple and Temple Church, London

The order's history as a military and religious organization meant that many of these buildings blended the need for strong defense with the need for religious reverence. They remain among the most striking and stunning examples of medieval construction in the world.

The legacy of the Knights Templar has also been felt in the world of literature. One of the best loved books from the last century, Umberto Eco's 'Foucault's Pendulum' deals with the Templars as a central tenet of the storyline. Throughout the text, Eco blends his own research with invented conspiracy theories.

While it may not be based on fact, it does show the extent to which people are still willing to buy into stories about the Templars, and it reiterates that their fame and legacy has long outlived their organization. Just as books such as this one are still being written about the Knights Templar, people are still desperate to know more about such a dark, twisted, and secretive organization.

Conclusion

There are few organizations in the history of the world who have had as big an impact, relative to their size, as the Knights Templar. Not only did they establish a name and organization that is still recognized today, but they rose to become one of the key forces on the geopolitical scale. Their influence was felt on a national level and the banking system they helped invent became so successful that it ultimately led to their downfall.

With an organization such as this, it is to be expected that we should see so many theories and secrets put forward. Because the order themselves reveled in the secrecy and the clandestine nature of their society, it should come as no surprise to see that people have attempted to fill the void with rational explanations.

But beyond the intrigue, it is important to note the violence that followed the Templars. They were forged in the cradle of the Crusades, one of Christendom's most bloodthirsty, violent, and shameful moments. They came to embody the fight for the Holy Land and eventually met their demise in an equally sinister, twisted manner. Even when we're trying to discover more about the organization, the amount of people who died at their hands, or because of an association with the order should not be forgotten.

If you would like to discover more, there is a further reading section at the end of this book. For those who are seeking the full truth behind the Knights Templar, we may never know exactly what they had to hide. Until such time as we might know the entire truth, we will have to exist – much like the Templars themselves – in a world of myth, rumors, and lies.

Further Reading

Baigent, M. and Leigh, R. (1998). *The Temple and the Lodge*. London: Arrow.

Baigent, M., Leigh, R. and Lincoln, H. (2006). *The Holy Blood and the Holy Grail*. London: Arrow.

Carroll, R. and Prickett, S. (2008). *The Bible*. Oxford: Oxford University Press.

Chaumeil, J. (2010). *The Priory of Sion*. London: Avalonia.

Christopher, P. (n.d.). *Lost City of the Templars*.

Eco, U. (2001). *Foucault's Pendulum*. London: Vintage.

Haag, M. (2009). *The Templars*. London: Profile.

Hancock, G. (2001). *The Sign and the Seal*. London: Arrow.

Hodge, S. (n.d.). *Secrets of the Knights Templar*.

Howells, R. (2011). *Inside the Priory of Sion*. London: Watkins Pub.

Martin, S. (n.d.). *The Knights Templar*.

Nicholson, H. (2010). *The Knights Templar*. Philadelphia: Running Press.

Robinson, J. (1989). *Born in Blood.* New York: M. Evans & Co.

Smith, U. (n.d.). *Daniel and the Revelation.* Nashville, TN: Southern Publishing Assoc.

About the author

Conrad Bauer is passionate about everything paranormal, unexplained, mysterious, and terrifying. It comes from his childhood and the famous stories his grandfather used to tell the family during summer vacation camping trips. He vividly remembers his grandfather sitting around the fire with new stories to tell everyone who would gather around and listen. His favorites were about the paranormal, including ghost stories, haunted houses, strange places, and paranormal occurrences.

Bauer is an adventurous traveller who has gone to many places in search of the unexplained and paranormal. He has been researching the paranormal and what scares people for more than four decades. He also loves to dig into period of history that are still full of mysteries, being an avid reader of the mystic secret societies that have mark history and remain fascinating and legendary throughout the times.

He has accumulated a solid expertise and knowledge that he now shares through his books with his readers and followers. Conrad, now retired, lives in the countryside in Ireland with his wife and two dogs.

More Books from Conrad Bauer

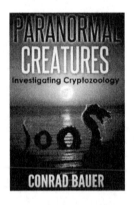

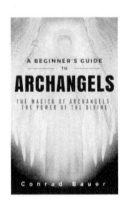

Printed in Great Britain
by Amazon